BASIC STUDIES

IN

SOTERIOLOGY

by: David A. Shortt

Copyright © 2005 by David Allen

Basic Studies in Soteriology
by David Allen

Printed in the United States of America

ISBN 1-59781-473-3

All rights reserved solely by the author. The author guarantees all contents are original and do not infringe upon the legal rights of any other person or work. No part of this book may be reproduced in any form without the permission of the author. The views expressed in this book are not necessarily those of the publisher.

Unless otherwise indicated, Bible quotations are taken from the King James Version by Cambridge Publishers.

www.xulonpress.com

I dedicate this series of articles that makes up this booklet to my Pastor D.Paul Tuck Sr., Pastor of Landmark Baptist Church Richmond Hill who has encouraged me at a time when my life was at a low ebb and urged me to take an active part in setting up our web site Bible Institute (Landmark Baptist Bible Institute-Canada) including writing and putting together these articles into one book both for use in our Institute and for print. Thank you

This is a series of four articles on SOTERIOLOGY

1) REGENERATION 9
2) CONVERSION 37
3) SANCTIFICATION..53
4) ETERNAL SECURITY..75

REGENERATION

REGENERATION

INTRODUCTION:

We hear a lot of talk about regeneration and the need for it these days, but I wonder if people really know what they are talking about.

In this article I would like to:

1) Explain the meaning of regeneration
2) Explain the need for regeneration.
3) Explain man's incapability of regenerating himself.
4) Explain that regeneration is a work of God working in us - grace.

WHAT DOES REGENERATION MEAN?

The word itself tells a lot. To generate means the holding of power, or being filled with power. Hence when something is regenerated it implies that whatever had had power somehow lost that power and by regenerating it, it had been re-filled with power. A good example would be a car battery that had been full of power and had run down through use and needed the power replaced. So it was charged up again - or in other words - regenerated, refilled with power.

But what has this to do with man - how does this fit into us and salvation and our walk with God? The answer is - everything. The

Bible makes it clear that unless we are regenerated there is no hope of us ever coming to Christ, or in being obedient to His demands. But of course we are not talking about the kind of power a battery would have. We are talking about life - spiritual life - which is in addition to the physical life which enables our physical body to function. Just as the physical body needs power - life as we are accustomed to, if we want to operate in the spiritual world we must have a spiritual life, or as the Bible refers to it at times - a new nature.

It is the entering into our heart of this spiritual nature that is called regeneration - it is also called being born again. We have been born again with a second nature giving us two natures. One of these natures - our human nature received from our parents dating back to Adam and Eve still wants to carry on doing the things our human nature likes to do. This is always contrary to what God wants, and this causes us to always be doing things against God's laws - this is called sin. On the other hand the other nature is God's nature - and of course since it is God's nature this nature wants to do what God wants, and its influence in us will be to cause us to do what God wants and be obedient to His laws. There is a constant battle between these two natures so that one moment a person can be a Godly, pious person, the next, that same person may be anything but godly and pious. Why? probably because he has been offended in some way and that human nature in us wants to retaliate in this ungodly manner. This unfortunately will be the way we Christian will be as long as we are in the flesh.

There are scriptures that support what I have been saying but I will not go to them at this point, but I surely will as we progress into our study.

WHY DOES ONE NEED REGENERATION?

To understand fully why one has to be regenerated we must go right back to the beginning. As I have already stated regenerated implies that at one time we had power, and lost it some how, so regeneration is having this power we lost restored.

In the beginning God created mankind with body, soul and spirit. Like the three parts of the Godhead each part has its own job in their existence.

Let's examine them

1) **Our Body:** the physical part of us - since it is only physical it needs life to make it function. It can do nothing in regards believing or not believing in things spiritual. It just does as its told by the "soul" part of us.

2) **Our soul:** This is our human nature that drives our physical body. It is what make us who we are, makes us think the way we do, act the way we do. This part of us is non-compatible with the spirit of God. It is at enmity with God and just can not think a good thought toward God in itself. The soul may cause us to be religious and have a form of godliness but if looked at through God's eyes their seemingly good works are nothing but a pile of filthy rags.

So - to understand or have any kind of relationship with God - or to be able to do any good - we must have that third element:

3) **Holy Spirit:** This is God's spirit in us humans that gives us the ability to respond to God in any way shape or form. Without this Holy Spirit God would mean very little to us - in fact nothing, just a word we can toss around at will and someone we can shout for in an emergency or a name to use in vain when hurt or angered.

Our original parents were created with all three elements. That's why they could live and talk with God in person in the Garden of Eden.
But then something happened that resulted in our Fore-parents losing one of the elements. The most important one of all - The Holy Spirit element that allowed them to have fellowship and companionship with God.
You remember the story of how Satan met Eve in the Garden - out of the presence and influence of God, how he tempted her into

eating of the forbidden fruit. How he caused doubt in her mind towards God by questioning the validity of God's threat to whether God would cause them to die as a result of taking that fruit. Satan made a liar of God. He said they would not die as God had said, but would be as a god herself if she ate of that fruit. Of course Eve fell for it wanting to be a God. Then she went to her husband, Adam and convinced him to eating the fruit using much the same argument as Satan had on her.. And of course Adam not wanting to lose his wife, ate the forbidden fruit. The problem was that that chief of liars, Satan did not tell Eve the whole story. He implied without saying it that they would not die. Satan was deceiving her as usual, He implied that God was talking about dying physically only. But God did not just mean physically when He had told Adam of this fruit and to leave it alone. When God refers to death He usually means spiritual death - or separation from God. When He told Adam he would die if he ate of that fruit He meant he would die in two ways - first spiritually, then physically. But satan implied that God was only talking about death in the one sense - physically, and in fact stated that in reality God is telling them a lie - they really wouldn't die if they ate that fruit, instead they would become like gods, knowing good and evil. Let's read
this scripture -

> ***GENESIS 3:1-5*** *—- Now the serpent was more subtle than any beast of the field which the Lord God had made. and he said unto the woman, Yea, hath God said, Ye shall not eat of every tree of the garden? And the woman said unto the serpent, we may eat of the fruit of trees of the garden: but of the fruit of the tree which is in the midst of the garden, God hath said, Ye shall not eat of it, neither shall Ye touch it, lest Ye die. And the serpent said unto the woman, Ye shall not surely die: For God doth know that in the day Ye eat thereof, then your eyes shall be opened, and Ye shall be as gods, knowing good and evil.*

And they did die spiritually - immediately on God confronting them about the matter. They were immediately banned from the

Garden of Eden and they both lost any communication with God after that, because that third element - God's Holy Spirit in us now became inactive, or dead to them. And to us, their descendants since then. We have lost any fellowship, companionship, or understanding of God or things pertaining to God until God chooses to regenerate a person and restores that spiritual element within us. But even then not to the same degree Adam and Even had. That element will not be as strong in us until after death when we return to God in our eternal body.

After Adam and Eve had eaten that forbidden fruit they must have thought for many years that Satan was right. They did not die immediately - physically. They lived until they were over 800 years old. That is an awful long time. But in God's own time they did die, which proves God's promises will be kept - always, in His own time and purpose.

How did this fall of Adam and Eve leave them spiritually? On being banned from the Garden of Eden Adam and Eve became spiritually dead. The Spiritual element in them was taken from them. The part of them that gave them communication with God. Now they were unable to communicate in any way in a spiritual sense. And this is so with every one of their descendants that has ever been born. We are all spiritually dead. We have no Holy Spirit element in us, and that is the very element that we need if we are to be able to understand anything of a spiritual nature.

We cannot even want to believe in God, we can not even want to be obedient to God in a true sense. We may be willing to follow A God, but not THE God of the Bible, but only the many other gods that people worship in our world today. Even most who do claim to worship the God of the Bible do not worship in the way OF the Bible, therefore their claim is not valid and do not have the God of the Bible any more than those who do not even know the existence of the God of the Bible. Only God regenerated people can come to the true God in belief and obedience.

Are you starting to get the idea of just how important being regenerated is?

MAN'S INABILITY

Now let's start looking at a few scripture. Let's take a look at how God sees us, just how incapable we are of doing anything pleasing to God.

We will start our search by looking at these scriptures, let's start in the Old Testament:

<u>ISAIAH 64: 6-7</u> — *But we are all as an unclean thing, and all our righteousness are as filthy rags: and we all do fade as a leaf: and our iniquities, like the wind, have taken us away. And <u>there is none that calleth upon thy name, that stirreth up himself to take hold of thee:</u> for thou hast hid thy face from us, and has consumed us, because of our iniquities.*

There is none that can stir up himself to believe in God, or in any way be obedient to God. That puts us in an awful predicament doesn't it? Let's look further in how God sees us. We might see ourselves and our fellow man as good, or at least see some good in us all - but the above and what follows will make it plain that God sees us differently. Let's get one thing straight - a barrier of sin is between us and God - SIN - and we all are sinners in God's sight.

Now let's go to the New Testament and have a look there at how God sees us:

<u>ROMANS 3:23</u> — *For all have sinned, and come short of the glory of God.*

Now note what happens to a person once they have sinned even once.

<u>JAMES 2:10</u> — *For whosoever shall keep the whole law, and yet OFFEND in <u>ONE</u> point, he <u>is GUILTY of ALL.</u>*

From this scripture we see clearly that all we have to do is break one of God's laws and as far as God is concerned we have broken them all - all the time. Can anyone say that they have never broken one of God's commandments? This is not just talking about the ten commandments - it is referring to anytime God say "do this" and we do not do what He says - or if God says "do not do that" - and we do it anyway - you are breaking God's commandments - you are being disobedient to God - you are guilty of sin.

You only have to sin once and you have lost all chance of obtaining salvation by any works of your own. You have lost your innocence and became a guilty sinner - a candidate for hell, not heaven. You will have to turn to the completed works of Jesus Christ.

Now let's look at what happens to those who sin:

EZEKIEL 18:20— The soul that sinneth, it shall die.

Sin is what brought death to all mankind through Adam and Eve as we have already read. They were the first sinners, but since we are their children we have inherited their sin nature which is under the bondage of sin. It cannot help but sin - therefore we are sinners by nature. We do not die because of Adam and Eve's sin, although it is true we did inherit their sinful nature, but still we die as a result of our own sins. This death is of course in two stages - first we die physically. We all know that some day we will die. All this is a result of our first parents sins, who we get our own sinful nature from, that causes us to sin - and also we are under the curse of the second death - spiritual death - separation from God.

This is the situation we find ourselves in. We are dead in trespasses and sin. We are separated from God and we cannot even want to know anything of the God of the Bible, anymore than a physically dead person can know about, or want to know anything of life in the physical sense. This may be hard to understand - since we are living creatures with a thinking brain. Yet we are not able to come to any understanding ourselves of spiritual things. This fact is of great offense to the natural mind. That is true - we can be very intelligent in an intellectual way, the very smartest in our physical world, but in the spiritual world be absolutely dead - unable to comprehend anything - know anything of a spiritual nature.
Let's see what God says about human wisdom:

<u>1 CORINTHIANS 1:19-29</u> — For it is written, I will destroy the wisdom of the wise, and will bring to nothing the understanding of the prudent. Where is the wise? where is the scribe? where is the dissipater of this world? hath not God made foolish the wisdom of this world? For after that in the wisdom of God the world by wisdom knew not God, it pleased God by the foolishness of preaching to save them that believe. For the Jews require a sign, and the Greeks seek after wisdom: but we preach Christ crucified, unto the Jews a stumbling block, and unto the Greeks foolishness; But unto them which are called, both Jews and Greeks, Christ the power of God, and the wisdom of God. Because the foolishness of God is wiser than men; and the weakness of God is stronger than men. For Ye see your calling, brethren, how that not many wise men after the flesh, not many mighty, not many noble, are called; but God hath chosen the foolish things of the world to confound the wise; and God hath chosen the weak things of the world to confound the things which are mighty; and base things of the world, and things which are mighty; and base things of the world, and things which are despised, hath God chosen, Yea, and things which are not, to bring to naught things that are: that no flesh should glory in His presence.

Note that the last verse states that God has no respect to those who are wise in there human mind - their wisdom means nothing to God, a mind that is not able to comprehend God or anything of a spiritual nature. let's read some more.

<u>1 CORINTHIANS 3:18-21</u>— Let no man deceive himself, if any man among you Seemeth to be wise in this world, let him become a fool, that he may be wise, for the wisdom of this world is foolishness with God. For it is written, He taketh the wise in their own craftiness. And again, the Lord knoweth the thoughts of the wise, that they are vain, Therefore let no man glory in men.

Human wisdom will never understand - is just not compatible with spiritual wisdom. Human wisdom is of the world, of the physical. Spiritual wisdom is from God only. No one by nature has that spiritual wisdom - it is put in us if and as God so pleases. I will say more of that later in this lesson. The following scripture will explain why we are in the state we are:

***EPHESIANS 2:1** — And you hath He quickened, who were DEAD in trespasses and sins.*

and

***EPHESIANS 2:5** — Even when we were DEAD in sins, hath quickened us together with Christ.*

***COLOSSIANS 2:13** — And you, being dead in your sins and the un-circumcision of your flesh, hath he quickened together with him, having forgiven you all trespasses.*

We see from these scriptures that in our natural state - the way we are born from our parents we are spiritually dead. The third element that Adam and Eve had in them - the spirit element - is now not in us as it was in them to begin with - but "died" - or became inactive in them - as a result of their sin. Let's take a look at more scripture to get a better picture of us all in our natural state - what our human nature is like:

***ROMANS 3:9-20** — What then? are we better than they? No, in no wise: for we have before proved both Jews and Gentiles, that they are all under sin; As it is written, there is none righteous no, not one: There is none that understandeth, there is none that seeketh after God. they are all gone out of the way, they are together become unprofitable; there is none that doeth good, no, not one. Their throat is an open sepulcher; with their tongues they have used deceit; the poison of asps is under their lips: Whose mouth is full of cursing and bitterness: their feet are swift* *to shed blood: Destruction and misery are in their ways: and the way of peace have they not known: there is no fear of God before their eyes. Now we know that what things-so-ever the law saith, it saith to them who are under the law: that every mouth may be stopped, and all the world may become guilty before God. Therefore by the deeds of the law there shall no flesh be justified in His sight: for by the law is the knowledge of sin.*

This is not a pretty picture of man and his nature is it? But it is what we are, and it is for this reason that it states in the last verse quoted that no man will ever get to heaven by keeping the law. We can never keep it to God's satisfaction. Remember **James 2:10** - if we even break one of God's commandments we cannot expect to get to heaven by our own works. The law was never - ever intended as a channel by which we obtain access to heaven. As stated in the verses quoted above it was meant only as a schoolmaster - a teacher to teach us why we needed someone else to do our goods works for us - and in addition - take the punishment due us and suffer for us.

Let's look at a few more scripture to show us that in our own nature we just can not be good enough to satisfy God.

ROMANS 8:7 — Because the carnal mind is enmity against God: for it is not subject to the law of God, neither indeed can be.

Our natural human mind is at enmity against God. That is very serious state. Enmity is a worse state than just plain enemies. It is an ingrained hatred that is impossible on our own to rectify. In this state our mind is not subject - or in any way capable of understanding, or able to keep the law anywhere near to God's satisfaction. That is very plain - but very offensive to the human mind, and is a cause in itself for the enmity between us and God.

This is why it is stated in:

1 CORINTHIANS 1:18 — **For the preaching of the cross is to them that perish foolishness: but unto us which are saved it is the power of God.**

1 CORINTHIANS 2:14 — But the natural man receiveth not the things of the spirit of God; for they are foolishness unto him: neither can he know them, because they are spiritually discerned.

But, you say, If a person cannot come to God because our human nature cannot understand the need for doing so, and does not want to accept a Savior and substitute when they cannot understand the need - how does one come to Christ, and why? If a person has been brought to the understanding of his spiritual position before God, then there must be something going on in that person's heart - a work of God. More on that later..

Let's look first and make it very clear that we are not saved by any works of our own - and why. Here is some scripture that tells us this as plainly as words can put it.

GALATIANS 2:16 — Knowing that a man is not justified by the works of the law, but by the faith OF Jesus Christ, even we have believed in Jesus Christ, that we might be justified by the faith OF CHRIST, and not by the works of the law: for by the works of the law shall no flesh be justified.

GALATIANS 3:11 — But that no man is justified by the law in the sight of God, it is evident: for The just shall live by faith.

It would be a good idea to read the whole chapters here to get a full picture of what the writer (indirectly the Holy Spirit) is saying. If we do - we all would have to come to the same conclusion Paul writes in:

ROMANS 3:28 — *Therefore we conclude that a man is justified by faith WITHOUT the deeds of the law.*

After reading all we have said about the condition of our human nature and it's inability to communicate with God in any way we must by now realize it would be disastrous to leave it up to our human ability to come to Christ or leave it up to our good works to pacify God with hopes of these good works obtaining salvation for us. No - it is so plainly put that our works have NOTHING to do with our getting to heaven. Instead, God has decreed that it is by putting our faith in the works of JESUS CHRIST that He has done FOR US that gets us to heaven. If you will note closely the verse I have already quoted above - this faith that enables us to trust in the finished work Christ has done for us is not our own - but the "faith **OF** Jesus Christ".

Let's go over that verse again.

GALATIANS 2:16 — *Knowing that a man is not justified by the works of the law, but by the faith **OF** Jesus Christ, even we have believed in Jesus Christ, that we might be justified by the - faith - **OF** - Christ, and not by the works of the law: for by the works of the law shall NO flesh be justified.*

Who does the faith belong to? It belongs to - or comes from - Jesus Christ. Remember way back in this lesson I quoted **Isaiah 64:6-7** - let's repeat it for emphasis here:

ISAIAH 64:6-7 — *But we are all as an unclean thing, and all our righteousnesses are as filth rags; and we all do fade as a leaf; and our iniquities, like the wind, have taken us away. And THERE IS NONE THAT CALLETH UPON THY NAME, THAT STIRRETH UP HIMSELF TO TAKE HOLD OF THEE: for thou hast hid thy face from us, and has consumed us, because of our iniquities*

JOHN 6:44 & JOHN 6:65 — *NO man can come to me, except the Father which hath sent me draw him: and I will raise him up at the last day. (6:65) And He said, Therefore said I unto you, that no man can come unto me, except it were given unto him of my Father.*

It is the entrance of God's Holy spirit in us that is the enabling power that allows us to come to Jesus Christ.

Isn't this totally consistent with what we have read elsewhere? This gives the reason why it must be the faith OF JESUS CHRIST in us that stirs us up to have faith in Jesus Christ, and not ourselves - as is so plainly stated in ***Galatians 2:16.*** God's word does not contradict itself - only man's beliefs do. Here we have two scriptures - one in the Old Testament and one in the New Testament talking about two different things yet totally consistent with what the other says. Let's look at some more scripture that is in total agreement with these two scriptures.

EPHESIANS 2:8-10— *For by grace are Ye saved through faith, and not that of yourselves, it is the gift of God - not of works lest any man should boast. For we are His workmanship created in Christ Jesus unto good works, which God hath before ordained that we should walk in them.*

These few verses tell us a great deal.

1) that our salvation has nothing to do with any work on our part - instead it comes through the grace of God

2) Salvation is a gift, given to us at God's pleasure.

3) Salvation is not of works because if it was people would go about boasting of the good works they were doing. We see plenty of that as it is!!

4) It goes on to say we our Gods workmanship - or piece of art, He makes us as he pleases, creating us in Christ Jesus unto -

or for the purpose of good works.

5) All this was before ordained that we should walk in these good works. Not maybe, as some try to tell us, but for the purpose of and unequivocally will, for when God sets a purpose and decrees something to happen - it will happen in God's own time.

Isn't this totally consistent with scriptures again? Lets look at a couple. just to confirm this is indeed in agreement with scripture in:

***ISAIAH 64:8** — But now, O Lord, thou are our father: we are the clay, and thou our potter: and we all are the work of they hand.*

***ROMANS 9:20-21** — Thou will say then unto me, why doth He yet find fault? for who hath resisted His will? Nay but, O man, who art thou that replies against God? Shall the thing formed say to him that formed it, why has thou made me thus? Hath not the potter power over the clay of the same lump to make on vessel unto honor, and another unto dishonor*.

These verses very emphatically remind us that we are the creation of God and since He is the artist that has formed the piece of art then He has a right to do with us as He sees fit. We may not like it, but what can we do about it? Get mad - have a temper tantrum and say I am not going to worship a God like that? I assure you if you do - you will be the loser - not God. The best thing to do is just accept God as the supreme being of the universe and we just a weak member of His creation, and accept what He has in store for us. We may have some rough water in store for us in this world, but in the next - out in eternity - the good He has in store for us will so out shine our rough waters here it will make everything here all worthwhile. Keep that in mind by faith and this life will not seem so unfair.

Since we are just a weak member of God's creation that can do nothing unless God wills it then He must have a plan. What is it and where did it all start.

That assumption is absolutely correct. God does have a plan and that plan met its final decree at God's determinate council way back in eternity before time ever began. We see this in:

***ACTS 2:23** — Him, being delivered by the determinate council and foreknowledge of God, Ye hath taken, and by wicked hands have crucified and slain.*

This of course is talking about Jesus being delivered into the hands of the Romans by the Jewish leadership and being slain on the cross. That was no accident - it was all part of God's plan for this part of His creation.

His plan is also explained in very general terms in the following scripture:

***ROMANS 8:28-29** — And we know that all things work together for good to them that love God, to them who are the called according to HIS purpose. For whom He did foreknow, HE also did predestinate to be conformed to the image of His Son, that He might be the firstborn among many brethren. Moreover whom He did predestinate, them He also called: and whom He called, them He also justified: and whom He justified, them he also glorified.*

Yes God knew from as far back in eternity as He Himself existed what He was going to do. At this determinate council all His plans were finalized and set in motion exactly as He had planned all along. Since God is unchangeable, what His purpose is now it always has been, then this must be so. On the basis of His foreknowing of what He was going to do He set the plans in motion to carry out those plans. We are all part of those plans and although we do not know fully what they are - we might even try to thwart them, but it can't be done. Not even by Satan who is for ever trying to thwart God's plans.

Let's look at only one more scripture to confirm that God has always known what He was going to do. This one is found in:

ACTS 15:18 — *Known unto God are all His works from the beginning of the age.*

Let's now search the scripture and see if we can't piece together some of this plan God has set out for mankind and regeneration which results in our salvation.

Let's start from the beginning. Way back in the Old Testament even we can see from statements made that God has a plan and events that unfold are events determined at His determinate counsel. He at times gives us a little glimpse into those plans and how He operates.

One of these is found in:

GOD'S PROMISE OF A NEW SPIRIT

EZEKIEL 36:26-27 — *A new heart also will I give you, and a new spirit will I put within you: and I will take away the stony heart out of your flesh, and I will give you an heart of flesh. And I will put my spirit within you, and cause you to walk in my statutes, and Ye shall keep my judgments, etc.*

We have read from several scriptures before this that it is impossible for us in our hopelessly sinful nature to understand, or ever have any kind of compatibility with the things of God. We are unable to come to God and ask for salvation due to this sinful nature that cannot like God or His ways - only the kind of life our human nature likes, which in every way is contrary to the kind of life God demands. If this is the case - and as we have read over and over - it is, then how do we come to God? How do we become a believer - a follower of Jesus Christ?

Ezekiel 36:26&27 gives the answer. God makes the difference in the one being saved. How? He puts another spirit in us. His own Holy Spirit takes up residence in our heart - the part of us that makes us what we are and the individual we are.

This is the experience that is called being "BORN AGAIN" in the New Testament.

Another term - the term which we are studying is - regeneration. Remember I stated at the beginning that when Adam and Eve was created they had three elements to their makeup. They consisted of - body, soul and Holy spirit. But when they were cast from the Garden of Eden they died spiritually, which meant they lost the Holy spirit element part of them. As a result they lost communication with God and all the privileges that went with that. Every human since has been like that, no Holy spirit element in us that can give us insight into the things of God. That's why the scriptures that we looked up that shows us our hopeless status before God in our human depravity - and is doing the job of a "schoolmaster" - teaching us that we cannot measure up to God's demands - that we MUST look to another who can and did meet all the demands of God - the Lord Jesus Christ.

THE IMPORTANCE OF THE NEW SPIRIT BEING BORN WITHIN US

How important is this experience of God empowering us with this Holy spirit that He promised us in **Ezekiel 36:26&27**? Absolutely essential - as we will read in **John 3:3**. Let's go there.

***JOHN 3:3** — Jesus answered and said unto him, verily, verily, I say unto thee, except a man be born again, he cannot see the kingdom of God.*

You should read all that is said there about the importance of this new birth referred to here and many other places as - being born again, and in other places as being - regenerated. You MUST be born again of this Holy spirit - the very Holy spirit that is mentioned in **Ezekiel 36** or you CANNOT see - or comprehend, or understand anything of the kingdom of God. And if you cannot comprehend - or under stand - anything of the kingdom of God - or spiritual things, you certainly will never enter and see the kingdom of God in a physical sense. In other words you will never enter heaven.

As I have already mentioned - this experience of having the Holy Spirit enter us and take up residence in us is called regeneration. If you recall at the first of this article I said the meaning of regeneration means that at one time we had been "generated" - or had power, but lost it. Now we are regenerated - we get that power back again. We have that third element that Adam and Eve had - the Holy Spirit. That is the power Adam and Eve lost when cast from the Garden of Eve. We now regain that third element when we are regenerated - or another word for it - born again with this new Holy spirit. We are regenerated - we have power, the Holy Spirit is in us. But we do not have the full amount of faith Adam and Eve enjoyed. They did not sin while in the Garden of Eden up until the encounter with Satan. That was the one and only sin in the Garden. And that illustrates graphically that it only takes ONE sin to separate us from God eternally just as **James 2:10** says. Then they were cast out of the Garden and all mankind has sinned since then. We do sin - a life full of sin. So it is obvious we do not have the full amount of the Holy Spirit they had. But we do get a certain amount of the Holy Spirit's power dwelling in us. As noted in **John 3:3**, being born with this new spirit is absolutely essential if we are ever to see God - either with the spiritual eye or enter heaven for eternity.

Let's take a look at the following scripture to see again how importance this new birth is;

> *<u>ROMANS 8:8-9</u> — So then they (the unsaved) - that are in the flesh cannot please God. but Ye (that are saved) are not in the flesh, but in the (Holy) Spirit, if so be that the (Holy) Spirit of God dwell in you. Now if any man HAVE NOT the Spirit of Christ(God), he is NONE OF HIS. (not one of God's people) and if Christ be in you, the body is dead because of sin; but the SPIRIT is LIFE because of righteousness. But if the spirit of Him (GOD) that raised up Jesus from the dead dwell in you, He that raised up Christ from the dead shall also quicken (make alive) your mortal bodies by His Spirit that DWELLETH IN YOU. VERSE 14 — For as many as are led by the Spirit of God(living in you), they are the sons of God.*

This makes it very, very clear that one must be born of God, or regenerated by God's Holy Spirit entering our heart and it is from the influence of that Holy Spirit that is now living in us where anything of a Godly nature comes from. Our faith, our believing in God, repentance, our obedience to the laws of God written or unwritten or even implied - all come from the influence of this Holy Spirit now living in us. Our own human nature could do none of these. That is why it is so essential for the quickening of God's holy spirit. Quickening is just the word that means exactly what we are talking about - to enter a person - and make that person spiritually alive - or to activate that person's spiritual element. Now one can think and act in a Godly manner because of the influence of God's Holy spirit living in us.

THE CHANGES IN US WROUGHT BY THE NEW BIRTH

Let's go to some scripture that will show us the change that takes place in our way of life. First let's look at 2 Corinthians:

<u>CORINTHIANS 5:17</u> — Therefore if any man be in Christ, he is a new creature; old things are passed away; behold, all things are become new.

This statement is very true. If a person has been born again of God, regenerated by the power of God's Holy Spirit living in him - then that person is a completely new creature. He now has two natures - a Holy nature from God plus we still have our old nature - our human nature. It goes on to say that old things have passed away. That is also very true. Our old way of thinking about God, our lifestyle and even our way of looking at the world about us changes. What we used to enjoy about the world and what they enjoy as entertainment, or pass time, suddenly does not seem as enjoyable anymore. A person who professes to be a Christian and continues on going to even the worst of shows, whether in a movie theater or live plays, or dances, or "out with the boys" going to beer parlors - or just continue to live a life that he always had is pretty solid evidence that the Holy Spirit of God is not dwelling in that person. God does not care for the lifestyle of man and will not allow us to continue on in such a style. A person with God's spirit dwelling within will also see through the phoniness of the world about them. There is much deception going on in this world. A person born of God knows that although he may not be able to detect all of the lies told in the media and in school, and by our politicians, they still can discern a lot more of the errors and wrongs of our society. A born again person will not believe all that is said by the worldly media.

Just one scripture to show how this influence affects a person: let's read:

1 JOHN 3:9-10 — Whosoever is BORN OF GOD doth NOT commit sin; for His seed REMAINETH in him: and he CANNOT sin; BECAUSE he is BORN OF GOD. In this the children of God are manifest, and the children of the devil: whosoever doeth NOT righteousness is NOT of God, neither he that loveth not his brother.

Whether we are a child of God or of Satan is manifested - or demonstrated to the world - by the kind of lifestyle we live. A child of God will live a life pleasing to God under the influence of God. (a righteous life). A child of Satan will NOT live a life pleasing to God but one that will please himself and his father - Satan - and the world because he does not have the influence of God in him - but the influence of Satan directing an unrighteous lifestyle.

The following scriptures will show very plainly the difference in lifestyle of a person who has been regenerated - born with a new nature abiding in him. We will start first with **Ephesians 2** where it tells us about the quickening of the Holy Spirit in us - then goes on to tell us what we all know about ourselves and the lifestyles we all once lived - then the change in our lifestyle when the Holy Spirit is born with in us.

EPHESIANS 2:1-5 — And you hath he quickened who were dead in trespasses and sins: Wherein in time past Ye walked according to the course of this world, according to

the prince of the power of the air, the spirit that now worketh in the children of disobedience Among whom also we all had our conversation (way of life) in times past in the lusts of our flesh, fulfilling the desires of the flesh and of the mind; and were by nature the children of wrath, even as others. BUT - God, who is rich in mercy, for His great love wherewith He loved us, Even when we were dead in sins, hath quickened us together with Christ, by grace Ye are save; And hath raised us up together, and made us sit together in heavenly places in Christ Jesus.

I don't think the language could be any clearer. He tells us of our old lifestyle which I don't think any of us can deny, then the change that the Holy spirit wrought in us when He quickened us.(made us alive - or activated Himself in us) And note very clearly what it was that made the changes. It was the Holy spirit that has now been activated in us that make all the changes in a saved person.

Nothing we did - we were dead spiritually - you don't have dead objects doing anything - spiritual or physical. Another verse that shows the difference that regeneration makes in found in **Galatians 5** - let's go there.

There are three things in this chapter I would like to point out.

1 - our lifestyle and our way of thinking before we are regenerated with the entrance of God's Holy spirit.
2 - although we Christians do have the Holy spirit dwelling in us we still will never be perfect as long as we are in the flesh.
3 - the Holy spirit dwelling in us does makes a big difference - but still not to perfection:

GALATIANS 5:19-21 — Now the works of the flesh are manifest which are these; adultery, fornication, uncleanness, lasciviousness, idolatry, witchcraft, hatred, variance, emulation's, wrath, strife, seditions, heresies, envyings murders, drunkenness, revellings, and such like: of the which I tell you before, as I have also told you

in time past, that they which do such things shall not inherit the kingdom of God.

The works of the flesh manifest - or are demonstrated by all these things - and are positive proof one does not have God's Holy spirit dwelling in them.

This is especially true if one's whole lifestyle is in this manner. We all have some sin in our nature and will succumb to that nature at times - but when we do we have a God influenced conscience that will drive us to repentance of our wrong doing. Go on to:

<u>VERSE 22</u> — *BUT - the fruit of the Spirit is love, joy, peace, long-suffering, gentleness, goodness, faith, meekness, temperance: against such there is no law.*

What is meant by the fruit of the spirit. Well, what is a fruit? A fruit of something is the result of a seed being planted is it not? - whether literally or figuratively. It is the results of some action that has been taken. Here in this scripture the fruit is the result of God's Holy Spirit that has been planted in our heart. That is why in other places this is also called "God's seed" in us. Such as **1 John 3** which we read earlier.

<u>GALATIANS 5:16-17</u> — *This I say then, walk in the Spirit, and Ye shall not fulfill the lust of the flesh. For the flesh lusteth against the spirit, and the Spirit against the flesh: and these are contrary the other: so that Ye cannot do the things that Ye would.*

<u>ROMANS 7:14-25</u> — **For we know that the law is spiritual: but I am carnal, sold under sin. For that which I do I allow not: for what I would, that do I not; but what I hate, that do I. If then I do that which I would not, I consent unto the law that it is good. Now then it is no more I that do it, but sin that dwelleth in me. For I know that in me (THAT IS, IN THE FLESH) dwelleth no good thing: for to will is present with me; but how to perform**

> **that which is good I find not. For the good that I would I do not: but the evil which I would not, that I do. Now if I do that I would not, it is no more I that do it, but sin that dwelleth in me. I find then a law, that, when I would do good, evil is present with me. or I delight in the law of God after the inward man: But I see another law in my members, warring against the law of my mind, and bringing me into captivity to the law of sin which is in my members. O wretched man that I am! who shall deliver me from the body of this death? I thank God through Jesus Christ our Lord. So then with he mind I myself serve the *law of God: but with the flesh the law of sin.***

This is what goes on between our old human nature - the old man - and God's Holy spirit that now abides in a Christian. The nature of God is not liked at all by our own human nature and fights it tooth and nail all the time. This will last as long as we are in the flesh. This is why Christians - even the best of us, are such good living, Godly people some time, and yet other times we are not at all Godly. Some even falling so low that God will take their life. But be very careful about this - God may take a Christian's physical life for a serious sin, but that does not affect his eternal spiritual life in any way.

A WARNING

Now that a person has been regenerated - or born again - whichever term one chooses to use it means that God's Holy spirit is now living within our heart. With the presence of this Holy spirit in our heart comes big changes in our life - right to the very core of our thinking - and that change of thinking will manifest itself in our lifestyle. It will change our likes - it will change our dislikes - it will change our habits - it will change our lifestyle - all for the good, in ways that fall into the category of a Godly way of living.

These changes are also going to be noticed by your relatives, friends and neighbors. You will soon notice a drifting away of most of these people from being your close buddies any more. Why?

because of your change of ways. You don't like the things they do any more like you used too, The entertainment you both used to like so much and maybe even used to attend, now is offensive to you, but not them. It is an old saying that: "birds of a feather flock together". But it is still as true today as the day it was first mouthed. You are no longer a bird of their flock - therefore they will not want you around them. It is heartbreaking - but you will soon realize your flock is not among them either - your bird of a feather is among other Christians who think and live as you do. You might even suffer verbal and even physical abuse from some of your acquaintances. Especially if you talk to them of what has happened to you. Expect all this - for we read that we will suffer as a result of our beliefs in God:

2 TIMOTHY 3:12 — *Yea, and all that will live godly in Christ Jesus SHALL suffer persecution.*

This is a rather clear promise from God that those who will stand up and be counted for the truth WILL suffer persecution. We know from history that that is true. The church of Rome put millions to death - people they called heretics - but in fact they were standing for the truth and the Roman Catholic church was the heretics. We Baptists suffered almost as much from the Protestants as we did from Rome. And not just from other so called Christians but from religions outside as well. The Muslims are terrible persecutors of Christians. The Buddhists have no love for Christians. Most religions persecute Christians in some form or other.

If people are left alone because they follow a popular belief it is no reason to think they are right in their belief. Rather, the ones that are being made fun of - ridiculed, bad mouthed - and some even to physical abuse - are more likely the ones that are right. Just to believe a doctrine because it is what most other churches believe just is not good enough in the eyes of the Lord. We must stick to "thus sayeth" the Lord".

CONCLUSION

We will close this study with this reminder:

TITUS 3:3-7— For we ourselves also were sometimes foolish, disobedient, deceived, serving divers lusts and pleasures, living in malice and envying, hateful, and hating one another. BUT - after that the kindness and love of God our Savior toward man appeared, not by works of righteousness which we have done, but according to His mercy He saved us, by the washing of regeneration and renewing of the Holy Ghost: Which He shed on us abundantly through Jesus Christ our Savior; That being justified by His grace, we should be made heirs according to the hope of eternal life.

This scripture is a quick review of all that has been said before. What our lifestyle was before - how God on His own initiative and nothing else regenerated us - or renewed the Holy Spirit in us, and then the change that came over our life as a result of this new Holy Spirit nature in us. Why? - that being justified by God's grace (that influence of Gods Holy Spirit in us) we will be made heirs according to the hope of eternal life.

Do your dear reader have this hope of eternal life? Do you feel the desire to learn more, to read, study, and get to know more of God's eternal life that is promised to those who will trust in all that Jesus has done for them and forget all that you have ever done as nothing but filthy rags in God's sight. If so you are probably already saved, or at least being called. The Holy Spirit is already at work and only needs that acknowledgment from you of what is going in you. Don't rebel - but humbly bow in acceptance of what God is doing in you - I assure you - you will never regret it!!

Amen - Praise God. God bless.

CONVERSION

CONVERSION

By: David Shortt

In this article I would like to study about conversion. What it is and how necessary it is for our expectation of living with God in an eternal life in a place called Heaven.

Why is it necessary for us to be converted? What are we being converted from and what are we being converted to? These are very important questions - so let's try to answer them.

First - Let's look at some scripture to see what the Holy Spirit tells us about conversion and its importance.

ACTS 15:3— And being brought on their way by the church, they passed through Phoenicia and Samaria, declaring the conversion of the Gentiles: and they caused great joy unto all the brethren.

It gave the Jewish brethren much joy to find out that many Gentiles were being converted to Jesus Christ along with themselves. As we know up until this time God dealt only with the Jewish nation. Generally - with very few exceptions, there were no saved people from among the Gentiles. But in our day, since Jesus came to this earth the first time this has changed. There is now salvation from among the Gentiles, that is salvation is open to every tongue and nation in this world. In fact for the time being, God is dealing more so from among the Gentiles than among the Jews. Let's look at some more scripture telling us that conversion is open to all races, colors and tongues (the whole world in general, but not without exception) is very important.

ACTS 3:19 — Repent Ye therefore, and be converted, that your sins may be blotted out, when the times of refreshing shall come from the presence of the Lord.

Here we are told to be converted and why - that your sins be blotted out. We will come back to this and study what is meant by this - our sins blotted out? What is He talking about?

Matthew 18:3— And said, verily I say unto you, Except Ye be converted, and become as little children, Ye shall not enter into the kingdom of heaven.

This is very strong language. If we are not converted from our sinful ways in order to have our sins blotted out as it said in the previous verse - we will never enter the kingdom of heaven. Note also that His audience consists of Gentiles as well as Jews.

If we go on into the next few verses it states clearly that one must become humbled - as humble as a small child is before their parents. Or in other words - as dependent on God and His work in and for us as a young child is dependent on their parents. We are all experienced enough in the realm of childhood - we know that a child is absolutely dependent on ones parents for continuation of their lives. They depend on their parents for food - drink - comfort and protection from other uncaring adults and even animals and even the elements around us. So we must come to the point in our lives that we realize to get into the kingdom of heaven we must stop looking at our own useless works and look to Jesus and His strength - and His accomplishments for us - and be as dependent on those works of Jesus as a young child is on his parents.

But let's step back some distance. Let's find out first why we need to be converted - and from what - to what. The first thing we must realize that each one of is a sinner in God's eyes. That these

sins we commit form an impregnable barrier between us and God that we cannot tear down ourselves. First - what is sin?
That is explained in:

1 JOHN 3:4 — Whosoever committeth sin transgresseth also the law: for sin is the transgression of the law.

I don't think that is too hard to understand. Anyone who transgresses the laws of God is a sinner in God's sight. Transgressor simply means a breaker of the law. We all do that - No one is exempt from this curse of breaking God's law. Even if we were just to include the ten commandments there is no one that has ever lived except the Lord Jesus Christ that has not broken at least one of those ten commandments. I really think an honest person would admit that they break a lot more than one of those commandments and much more than just once in his lifetime. That is all it takes is just one law broken once in our whole lifetime and we have sinned and our chance of getting to heaven on our own merit of good works has gone forever. Once we have broken just one law our status changes - changes from - being innocent of any wrong doing - to a guilty sinner. It does not make any difference how many sins, or how serious the sin was - you have broken God's law and you have now become a guilty sinner in God's eyes. No amount of pleading, begging, penitence, asking for forgiveness, or anything else will do any good.

But there is a way out of this dilemma which we will get to later. How do we know the above is true? The Bible tells us clearly in:

JAMES 2:10 — For whosoever shall keep the whole law, and yet offend in one point, he is guilty of all.

That is very plain language. If we keep the law totally and completely then make one mistake and break one title of a law - all hope is gone. Once we sin that puts us in a whole new status of life. Before we sinned that first sin we were innocent, free of guilt or wrong doing. Once we committed that first sin - it doesn't make any difference if we never committed another one the rest of our life -

whether we committed even one more, or we committed a zillion more - we are now guilty sinners. Nothing will ever change that now. WE ARE GUILTY SINNERS - PERIOD. That is why we believe in the total depravity of man. Once we have sinned our status is now - guilty sinner - it is absolutely impossible to change that.

All hope is gone.

EXCEPT ONE. Be converted to Jesus Christ and receive Him as your substitute. He has already kept the law to God's satisfaction and paid the penalty for those of us who do not. Every one of us humans have sinned so we all must look to the one who has not sinned and apply His righteousness to us. His righteousness He earned by His right living - living without sin. The only one who qualifies is the Lord Jesus Christ. All of us humans have sinned. We read this in:

ROMANS 3:23 — For all have sinned, and come short of the glory of God.

This verse clearly shows us our need of a savior. We all have sinned and came short of the standard God requires of us to get to heaven. We just will not make it by any effort we can muster up - how hard we work or how penitent we may become. There is only one way - let's look to another verse for that:

ROMANS 3:28 — Therefore we conclude that a man is justified by faith without the deeds of the law.

But what do we put our faith in? It is nice to talk about faith - but who or what do we put our faith in? Even if we understand we are helpless in ourselves to work out our own salvation it does not do much good to know this unless we understand that there is someone who has kept the laws of God and satisfied every one of God's demand of a perfect life in order for us to pass through heaven's door.

That is what I would like to do. Tell you of this person who so graciously did for us what we can not do for ourselves. That person is The Lord Jesus Christ. If I do and you come to believe fully that

Jesus Christ has done everything necessary for your for- giveness and to give you any chance at all of getting to heaven and you turn away from your own useless works and put your trust in what Jesus has already done then you will have been converted to Jesus Christ as God demands of each of us.

To Convert simply put means to persuade one to come over to your side. So if we are converted to Jesus Christ we are converted to Jesus Christ and His ways of doing things and we become followers of Him. At the same time we are converted **TO** Jesus Christ we are converted **FROM** oneself - our own self help efforts.

Let's find out a few things about Jesus that will help convict us that Jesus is not just another man who himself would be sinful and need of a Savior.

First and foremost we must realize Jesus is not just another sinful man, but is the Son of God who was sent by God to do for us what we couldn't do ourselves. Let's look at some scripture that shows that Jesus is accepted by God as the substitute that fulfilled His demands of the law and took our punishment on Himself in order that we would be free from any guilt of wrong doing (sin) or fear of punishment for them.

<u>MATTHEW 17:5</u> — While he yet spake, behold, a bright cloud overshadowed them: and behold a voice out of the cloud, which said, this is my beloved son, in whom I am well pleased: hear Ye him.

This leaves no doubt of God's approval of Jesus Christ and the work that He was doing, and how well He was doing it. So if Jesus Christ meets God's approval why shouldn't He meet ours?

Let's look up few scripture to see a little of the history of Jesus Christ. First off - it had been prophesied for centuries by Jewish prophets that there would be a Messiah - a special man of God - that would come to earth born of a virgin - that that person would be their leader and would lead the Jews back to God. In Matthew we read of the fulfillment of that prophecy whereby Jesus was conceived mirac- ulously by the Holy Spirit and thus Jesus was conceived and born not in a natural way but through a virgin. Mary was the mother chosen by God to carry that miraculously conceived child.

MATTHEW 1:18-25— Now the birth of Jesus Christ was on this wise: When as His mother Mary was espoused to Joseph, before they came together, she was found with child of the Holy Ghost. Then Joseph her husband, being a just man, and not willing to make her a public example, was minded to put her away privily. But while he thought on these things, behold, the angel of the lord appeared unto him in a dream, saying, Joseph, thou son of David, fear not to take unto thee Mary thy wife: for that which is conceived in her is of the Holy Ghost. And she shall bring forth a son, and thou shalt call His name Jesus: for He shall save His people from their sins. Now all this was done, that it might be fulfilled which was spoken of the Lord by the prophet, saying, Behold, a virgin shall be with child, and shall bring forth a son, and they shall call his name Emmanuel, which being interpreted is, God with us. Then Joseph being raised from sleep did as the angel of the lord had bidden him, and took unto him his wife: and knew her not till he had brought forth her first born son: and he called his name Jesus.

One of the places in scripture where it is prophesied that Jesus would be born of a virgin is:

Isaiah 7:14 — Therefore the Lord himself shall give you a sign: behold, a virgin shall conceive, and bear a son, and shall call his name Immanuel.

If we went on to chapter two of Matthew we would read there of the birth of Christ. The great Majestic son of God born in a lowly manger in a common barn meant for the habitat of Asses and other animals, some of God's lowest forms of His creation. This was to show his willingness to accept a lowly estate as He walked among the children of man - for the time being.

When we teach - or preach - what should we talk about? Well, of course it's good to talk about living a high moral life, or teach about the proper mode of baptism, or the Lord's supper. It is necessary to teach about the church - and many other Bible doctrines. But if you want people to be converted (won over to Christ - and saved) you must preach unto them Jesus. For a person to be saved they must be taught all the things pertaining to Jesus and His work to obtain our eternal destiny in heaven with Jesus. The following scripture will put in the proper prospective what is important when we preach to expect people to be saved:

ACTS 8:5-7 — Then Philip went down to the city of Samaria, and preached Christ unto them. And the people with one accord gave heed unto those things which Philip spake, hearing and seeing the miracles which he did.

ACTS 8:35 — Then Philip opened his mouth, and began at the same scripture, and preached unto him Jesus.

And the eunuch was saved as a result of this teaching of Jesus Christ.

LUKE 24:27 — And beginning at Moses and all the prophets, He expounded unto them in all the scriptures the things concerning Himself.

Once again there was a positive result of the preaching of Jesus Christ. This is what we must teach to unsaved if we expect them to be saved. Once saved and baptized into the church then all other doctrines should be taught them. That is the divine order Jesus laid out to His commission to His church in **Matthew 28:19-20**

This makes it clear that preaching Jesus Christ is what converts a spiritually dead, lost sinner to Jesus Christ. Not the teaching of high morals, or the proper method of baptism, or the Lord's supper - or any other of the many important doctrines of the Bible. Important yes, but only after one is saved. This does not mean we should not teach the law and its moral standard - just do not teach it to save people - but to instruct people in what God expects of us. The law never was meant to save - but to be a schoolmaster - teaching us what and where we go wrong and why we need to have Jesus Christ be our substitute and do things for us what we can't do ourselves - keep the law to God's standard.

ROMANS 3:20 — Therefore by the deeds of the law there shall no flesh be justified in His sight: for by the law is the knowledge of sin

GALATIANS 3:24 — Wherefore the law was our schoolmaster to bring us unto Christ, that we might be justified by faith

How does the law become our schoolmaster? It instructs us in the standard that God expects of us - and that not one single one of these laws can be broken or we have not met God's standard of conduct. It gives us something to compare our own life with. When we note God's standard then look at our own pitiable efforts to meet those standard we can soon see that there is no way that we can meet God's standard - absolutely no way. If that is the case - if we expect to get to heaven then we must look elsewhere for and hope we can find a substitute to do for us what we can't do for ourselves. We find Him in the Lord Jesus Christ - by faith in what the Lord Jesus has already done - it is not a case of He will do it someday - He already has.

There are many things about the Lord Jesus Christ that we should know about. We have already covered a couple of these. We have already mentioned that Jesus was conceived in a miraculous way through a special action of the Holy Spirit. This makes Jesus a God/Man. His mother was a woman which of course is part of mankind. But His father was God. (the Holy Spirit who is also God) If Jesus was born the natural way with a human father and mother He would be no better than you and me, having a sinful depraved human nature. And would sin like you and me because He could not fight His own nature anymore than any other man could. He would be man - not God/man and restricted to what we expect of man - sin.

Because Jesus had God's nature in Him He was not totally depraved as we who are fully human. He could turn away from sin when tempted. And He was tempted in many ways. In Matthew, Mark and Luke there is recorded where Jesus spent 40 days in the wilderness where Satan tried to influence (tempt) Jesus to sin. I will only quote the one passage.

MATTHEW 4:1-11 — Then was Jesus led up of the Spirit into the wilderness to be tempted of the devil. And when He had fasted forty days and forty nights, He was afterward an hungered And when the tempter came to Him He said, if thou be the son of God, command that these stones be made bread. But He answered and said, it is written, man shall not live by bread alone, but by every word that proceedeth out of the mouth of God. Then the devil taketh Him up into the holy city, and setteth Him on a pinnacle of the temple. And saith unto Him, if thou be the son of God, cast Thyself down: for it is written, He shall give His angels charge concerning thee: and in their hands they shall bear thee up, lest at any time thou dash thy foot against a stone. Jesus said unto him, it is written again, thou shalt not temp the Lord thy God. Again, the devil taketh Him up into an exceeding high mountain, and sheweth him all the kingdoms of the world, and the glory of them; and saith unto Him, all these things will I give Thee, if thou wilt fall down and worship me. then saith Jesus unto him, get thee hence, Satan: for it is written, thou shalt worship the Lord thy God, and him only shalt thou serve. Then the devil leaveth Him, and behold, angels came and ministered unto Him.

Here in the wilderness all alone with the devil Jesus was tempted to do evil as much or more than any man living before or after Him. Yet He failed not. He never broke one of God's laws in His life of 33 years. Let's read this in:

HEBREWS 2:18 — **For in that He Himself hath suffered being tempted, He is able to soccour them that are tempted.**

HEBREWS 4:15 — **For we have not an high priest which cannot be touched with the feeling of our infirmities; but was in all points tempted like as we are, yet without sin.**

No one can accuse Jesus of not knowing what we went through here in life. He experienced anything and everything a human could experience. And bore it quietly - for us, sinless to the end, that He may be qualified to say -

(A) - I have kept the law and all the demands of God. I am righteous in my own right - by my own efforts - therefore I hold out this offer - to those of you who will receive this offer I agree to make an exchange with you. I will put my righteousness to your account - and
(B) - At the same time I will take the burden of your sins upon me. I agree to take God's wrath off you and bear it myself. Therefore I will become the sinner in your stead and bear the punishment that is coming meant for you unless you receive this offer. This I will do by dying on the cross.

And this is exactly what Jesus does. To those who receives this offer God imputes (gives credit to) Jesus' right living (His righteousness) to us while at the same time He takes our sins on Himself and on Calvary's cross suffered the paid and suffering we would have received had we not received Jesus as our substitute to take all this in our place. Let's look at:

ROMANS 4:6-8 — **Even as David also describeth the blessedness of the man, unto whom God imputeth righteousness without works, saying, blessed are they whose iniquities are forgiven, and whose sins are covered. Blessed is the man to whom the Lord will not impute sin.**

Here we see how God imputes to us believer in Jesus - those of us who stop trusting in our own efforts and have put all our trust in Jesus and His work. This means that God put the righteousness that Jesus earned by His right living - the keeping of the law to God's satisfaction - on us. Since we now have the righteousness of Jesus in us then we are now as righteous (perfect) as Jesus Himself is. This is how our sins become forgiven and covered as mentioned in the verses quoted above. Why? - Because Jesus first gives us His own righteousness so we don't have to worry about earning our own - plus He died - suffering the penalty we would have suffered for our wrong doings if we had not been converted TO Christ - and AWAY from ourselves and our own useless efforts.

How was Jesus able to go through thirty three years of life without ever sinning once? This can only be answered by what we have already read about Jesus. He was not totally man. He was God/man. It was only through the Holy Spirit nature that Jesus had in full measure that He was able to live without sin. It is because we humans - even the best of us, even after we are born again of this Holy nature, we only have a measure of the Holy spirit in us. In other words God does not dwell in us in full completeness like He did Jesus. We still have our human nature. Jesus didn't. Therefore, since we still are plagued with our sinful human nature and with only a measure - a measure dished out as is pleasing to God - everyone being different - we will continue to have our failures as long as we are in this fleshly body. Once we are out of this fleshly body and in heaven we will get a full measure of faith (the Holy spirit). Let's read where these things are mentioned.

ROMANS 12:3 — For I say, through the grace given unto me, to every man that is among you, not to think of himself more highly than he ought to think; but to think soberly, according as God hath dealt to every man the measure of faith.

Paul himself admits to speaking Godly truths through the much grace (faith) God has bestowed on him. He knew that most men did not get this much grace bestowed on them - in fact, very few do.

EPHESIANS 4:7 — **But into every one of us is given grace (faith) according to the measure of the gift of Christ.**

As I said before - each person has his own measure of faith given to them by God at God's own pleasure. Some to become very knowledgeable in the things of God, others to a large extent left in the dark so to speak. Only God in His sovereignty knows why He deals as He does. But in the case of the Lord Jesus Christ there is no measure of faith. Jesus is God - no more needs to be said. Please go to:

JOHN 3:34 — **For He whom God hath sent speaketh the words of God: for God giveth not the spirit by measure unto Him**

These are all things one should know about Jesus if anyone is to be converted to the Lord Jesus. We must preach Jesus and all the things pertaining to Him if we expect to have any success in converting anyone from there self centered life depending on his own efforts to looking to and depending on what Jesus has already done for them. We Have already noted that:

1) Jesus was God - He was born by a woman but conceived by a special act of the Holy Spirit.

2) Because He was God and there no sinful nature in Him Jesus was able to live the sinless life that God demands of everyone.

3) Jesus not only gives us believers in Him - those converted to Him and is one of His faithful followers - His righteousness, but He took our unrighteousness on Himself and when He died on Calvary cross He was suffering the penalty for our sin we should be and would be had He not agreed to take our punishment on Himself.

4) He also suffered three days and three nights in the heart of the earth (hell) as part of that punishment God inflicted on Him for the sins WE committed.

MATTHEW 12:40 — **For as Jonas was three days and three nights in the whale's belly; so shall the Son of man be three days and three nights in the heart of the earth.**

5) Then Jesus arose from the dead - He did not stay in the grave as a normal man who has died would. He raised His own dead body from the grave and walked for another fifty days amongst His followers leading and guiding them in order to get His church started. His church had already been organized before these events took place - but it sort of got put on the back burner as the apostles wrestled for those three days Jesus was gone over what to do now. Jesus soon showed them what to do and until His ascension into the clouds about fifty days later, He lead them. But this time He did not leave them alone. He sent the comforter - The Holy Spirit - the third member of the Godhead to take over the leadership on earth of the Church that He had started. Let's read the following scriptures - it is good to read right from **John 15:18-26** - but I will only quote **John 15:26:**

JOHN 15:26 — **But the Comforter, which is the Holy Ghost, whom the Father will send in my name, He shall teach you all things, and bring all things to your remembrance, whatsoever I have said unto you**

Now Jesus is in heaven - He is still the head of His Church - with the Holy Spirit directing things from earth itself.

7) We should also know and never forget that now Jesus in heaven acting on the behalf of us believers before almighty God. God cannot look upon us sinners Himself - so Jesus acts as a mediator between us and God. Part of this mediator ship is to remind God that when we sin here on this life that we are now under His protection as a believer in Him. One who is depending of Jesus' efforts for salvation and not our own - so as a result God looks upon us as righteous as Jesus Himself is.

1 TIMOTHY 2:5 — For there is one God, and mediator between God and men, the man Christ Jesus

These are the things we must believe in. (trust in explicitly - put our spiritual life totally in His hands) When we are truly converted to Jesus Christ this is what we will do. Liken it to when we fly in an airplane. We believe in that pilot. We trust that he has taken the training to fly the plane and is capable of getting the plane off the ground - fly to our destination and land again. You think nothing of it - you believe in him. You trust him enough to put your life in his hand. You can't fly the plane yourself so you leave it to the pilot who can. I can imagine the reception you would receive if you went to the cockpit and tried giving the pilot a few pointers. You would very likely be very unceremoniously escorted back to your seat. Neither does God appreciate His creation trying to give him pointers and trying to "fly" the salvation plane themselves. God is the Pilot, He knows what He is doing - let Him do the flying. When you do - you know you will get to your destination. If you don't - you will end up at a totally different destination. Hell - for all eternity.

I pray that these lessons have helped you understand your position before God and the need to be converted to God and His ways, away from your own self help and to trust explicitly in the finished work of Jesus Christ.

SANCTIFICATION

SANCTIFICATION

By: David A. Shortt

INTRODUCTION:

In this series of lessons we will take a look at the doctrine of sanctification.

We will take a look at its meaning as used in the Bible and from there progress on to a more detailed study of when God sanctified and how it is applied to us.

THE MEANING OF SANCTIFICATION:

First it should be made clear that sanctification does not mean a second work of grace in our heart which makes those who achieve a high level of sanctification a sinless, perfect person - as some religious denominations try to tell us.

Let's take a look at a few scriptures to get the idea of what is meant by the word sanctify as used in the scriptures. Let's look at these verses:

EXODUS 13:2 — Sanctify unto me all the firstborn, whatsoever openeth the womb among the children of Israel, both of man and of beast: it is mine.

EXODUS 19:22 — let the priests also, which come near to the Lord, sanctify themselves, lest the lord break forth upon them

DEUTERONOMY 5:12 — Keep the Sabbath day to sanctify it, as the Lord thy God hath commanded thee.

I don't think there is too much doubt of the meaning of the word as used here. To set apart or separate . This is what sanctify means - to take an object out of a group of its own kind to be used for specified purpose.

GOD'S PURPOSE FOR US WHO ARE SANCTIFIED:
This is precisely what God wants to become of us - for us to be separated from the world and its ungodly system because He has a special purpose for us.

God wants us separated from the world - to be a very distinct people set apart from the worldly system we live in. This is clear from this verse:

1 PETER 2:9 — But Ye are a chosen generation, a royal priesthood, an holy nation, a peculiar people; that Ye should shew forth the praises of Him who hath called you out of darkness into His marvelous light.

Who is he talking to? That is made plain in:

1 PETER 1:1-2 — Peter, an apostle of Jesus Christ, TO THE STRANGERS scattered throughout Pontus, Galatia, Cappadocia, Asia, and Bithynia WHO ARE THE ELECT according to the foreknowledge of God the Father, through sanctification of the spirit, unto obedience and sprinkling of the blood of Jesus Christ.

Quite clearly it is Christians that is the subject being talked to. God Himself has sanctified us - or set us apart as a peculiar people belonging to Him with a design and purpose in mind for those who

He has set apart for His own use.

Clearly God has plans for us who He separates from the rest of the world and its ungodly system - plans that include working on His behalf in some capacity or another. One of these is to make a preacher out of us. But of course He does not make preachers out of us all. Let's look at a scripture that tells of a number of calls God calls us to - and these are not all of them:

EPHESIANS 4:11-12 — And He gave some, apostles, and some, prophets; and some, evangelists; and some, pastors and teachers; for the perfecting of the saints, for the work of the ministry, for the edifying of the of the body of Christ.

Clearly God took us out of the worldly system for a purpose - to do a job for Him and His work here in this world. As we read before - God does not expect us to carry on in the matters of this world's system as we did before. We are "New Creatures" in Christ now and the things we like to do and the things we enjoy doing are much different from what we enjoyed before God sought us out and made us one of His.

OUR DILEMMA:

Oh yes - we still live in this sin cursed world and can't eliminate all worldly activities or influence from our lives. To do so we would have to actually get off this world entirely. And that unfortunately we cannot do. Paul also says this is a problem - that to get away from the world and it's influence we would have to get out of this world - read:

1 CORINTHIANS 5:9-10 — I wrote unto you in an epistle not to company with fornicators; yet not altogether with the fornicators of this world, or with the covetous or extortioners, or with idolaters; for then must Ye needs go out of the world.

But even if we did get away from worldly influence we would

still be under the influence of our sinful depraved nature which we are unable to change.

What good would we be to the world if we did get out of it entirely, or even separated ourselves from the world so that we had no communication with it, like in convents or such like places of separation. We could not communicate to them the Gospel message - and that is one of the main jobs of God's called out ones - to teach others who have not yet heard it with the hopes that some of those we communicate with will also be ones whom God will call out. Just as he did us from a communication from someone we had with.

So as much as we would like to separate ourselves entirely from the bad influence of the world, until God takes us home to be with Him we will have to live and put up with a certain amount of worldly influence - good or bad - but coming from the world most of it is bad.

SEPARATE OURSELVES FROM THE WORLD:

But that does not mean we should willingly embrace and actively chase after the things the world in general likes - for if you go to the very next verse after the last verse we read it says this;

<u>1 CORINTHIANS 5:11</u> — But now I have written unto you not to keep company, if any man that is called a brother be a fornicator, or covetous, or an idolater, or a railer, or a drunkard, or an extortioner; with such an one no not to eat.

This is specifically telling us not to keep company with those who profess to be believers and yet do some of those thing you would expect from the unregenerate person - but certainly not from believers. But the context in general is that God does not expect us to live our lives out the same as the unregenerate - the unsaved who do not have God's holy spirit dwelling in them. If He did - He wouldn't tell us not to even eat with those professors who do keep on living as the world does. Why? Because if you keep your friends from among this kind of people you will spoil your own testimony of being one of God's called out ones. People of the world expect those who profess to be "born again" to be different too. If they see a professing Christian living as they are then their profession of faith does not mean much. They have ruined their credibility with the world. Any one associating with them will also spoil their reputation and credibility too.

So God says stay away from that kind of person.

2 CORINTHIANS 6:17 — Wherefore come out from among them, and be Ye separate, saith the lord, and touch not the unclean thing; and I will receive you.

Couldn't get any clearer than that. Stay away from as much as the worldly way of life as you can. We do have to brush shoulders with a lot of it - but not take it up as a lifestyle for yourself.

OUR OWN HISTORY:

We all come into this world as unbelievers - sinners. We lived among the people of this world loving the same things they do simply because we were one of them. We lived for the pleasing of the flesh and mind and were by nature the children of wrath. We were no different from anyone else that has walked this world of ours. Let's see how scripture agrees with this.

EPHESIANS 2:2-3 — Wherein in time past Ye walked according to the course of this world, according to the prince of the power of the air, the spirit that now worketh in the children of disobedience: Among whom also we all had our conversation (way of life) in times past in the lusts of our flesh, fulfilling the desires of the flesh and of the mind; and were by nature the children of wrath, even as others.

Isn't that a good description of each of our lives before God stepped in and made a difference in us? Let's go on to verse 5 of the scripture we were reading:

EPHESIANS 2:4-5 — **BUT GOD, who is rich in mercy, for His great love wherewith He loved us, even when we were dead in sins, hath quickened us together with Christ.**

BUT GOD stepped in and made a difference in our life. Note that it says while we were still dead in our sins - He did not wait to hear from us - any kind of cries from us. We couldn't, we were dead in sin - we didn't even know we needed life. But Got took the initiative and gave us spiritual life because it pleased Him to do so, and from this life God instilled in us comes the knowledge that we do need life from God as well as a Savior who will bear our burdens for us.

Note again that He says He loved us even when we were still "dead in sins" - or an unbeliever. This may be hard for the human intellect to grasp - but stop and think. God is a God that never changes. If He loves us now - He has always loved us - even as far back into eternity as He has existed. We know that has been forever. Since he loved us back in eternity then He loved us before we were born the first time. Then we are certain He loved us before we were born the second time. Since His love is eternal from past eternity to future eternity He had to love us during those sinful years of our life between the time we were born the first time and when we were born the second time. Those are the years of our sinful life. God knew we were a candidate for election to salvation - it just hadn't happened yet in reality.

His love did not just start when we in fact became saved - a found sheep. He loved us from way back in eternity when all these plans were just thoughts on His mind. So we see how that God did love us even during that period of time we were still in our sins.

God sanctifies us. He separates us from the world to be used as He sees fit in His work of salvation. Let's read:

2 THESSALONIANS 2:13 — **But we are bound to give thanks always to God for you, brethren, be loved of the lord, because God hath from the beginning chosen you to salvation through sanctification of the spirit and belief of the truth.**

There is a sequence of events that a person goes through. We were chosen back in eternity - sought out in life and through the preaching of the Gospel reached our hearts and used this method to draw us away from the world's system. Or he sanctified us.

THE DIFFERENCE WROUGHT IN US BY THE HOLY SPIRIT:

He does not separate us physically but in our thinking, our speech, our manner of life, our works reference the law, our likes, our dislikes will all change manifesting the work God has wrought in us. We are now a peculiar person - different from the rest of the world. How does He do this? As explained in verse one - the word used here and again in verse five is: quickened. God quickened those dead in sin. What does quicken mean? It means to give live - or activate life. And this is what God does.

We are all dead spiritually - in sin as these verses tell us, but God quickens us spiritually dead people - which makes us alive spiritually. We are no longer dead spiritually. We now have a living Holy spirit in us and this new living Holy spirit is going to have a very large influence in our life from this point on.

This new, Holy spirit will want to do what God wants instead of what our old human nature wants. It is God's Holy nature at work in us so it only stands to reason God's nature will want to do what God likes just as our human nature wants to do what our human nature likes.

Note closely here. God does not make anew our old nature. No - that stays the same old sinful, rebellious nature. But we are given a second nature - God's nature. These two natures are not friends with each other at all. In fact they are at odds with each other - always in conflict. Let's read that in:

<u>ROMANS 7:14-25</u> — For we know that the law is spiritual; but I am carnal, sold under sin. For that which I do I allow not; for what I would, that do I not; but what I hate, that do I. If then I do that which I would not, I consent unto the law that it is good. Now then it is no more I that do it, but sin that dwellth in me. For I know

that in me (that is, in my flesh,) dwelleth no good thing; for to will is present with me; but how to perform that which is good I find not. For the good that I would I do not; but the evil which I would not, that I do. Now if I do that I would not, it is no more I that do it, but sin that dwelleth in me. I find then a law, that, when I would do good, evil is present with me, For I delight in the law of God after the inward man: but I see another law in my members, warring against the law of my mind, and bringing me into captivity to the law of sin which is in my members.

GALATIANS 5:17 — **For the flesh lusteth against the spirit, and the spirit against the flesh: and these are contrary the one to the other; so that Ye cannot do the things that Ye would.**

If there was only one nature that had been renewed into a not so bad nature, then there could be no conflict with itself. But that is not what happens - God gives us a second nature and these two natures are in constant conflict. Our human nature wanting to do what human nature drives us to do, while the Nature of God drives us to do that which God wants.

This experience of the new nature being born within us is called being "born again". Our first birth of course being our physical birth with its human nature and now an altogether new nature from God is born within, which gives us a Holy nature in us as well.

This new Spirit is not something new God introduced in the New Testament. It is referred to as far back as Ezekiel's time. See what is said in the book:

EZEKIEL 36:26-27 —**A new heart also will I give you, and a new spirit will I put within you: and I will take away the stony heart out of your flesh, and I will give you an heart of flesh. And I will put my spirit within you, and cause you to walk in my statutes, and Ye shall keep my judgments, and do them.**

This new nature that God puts in a person that causes us to come to Him was known about for centuries before Christ's arrival on the scene. Then Christ confirmed the necessity of having that new Spirit (nature) born within us in order for us to have the ability to believe. This is recorded in:

JOHN 3:3 — Jesus answered and said unto him, verily, verily, I say unto thee, except a man be BORN AGAIN he cannot see the kingdom of God.

I repeat - except a man be born again, he cannot "see" (understand) comprehend) the things of God. And of course if you cannot see, or understand the things of God you will never enter the Kingdom of God. All with beautiful harmony with each other written centuries apart but agreeing with each other as if it was the same author wrote it all. Actually - It was - The Holy Spirit!!

The effect of this new nature God has planted in us is very obvious. It is what sanctifies us - or separates us from the world. Even if we do want to continue being friends with the world and to continue on as before - the world will soon not want to continue with us. Why? Because we have become so much different from them that they can not stand us in their presence. We will not have to come out from among them - they will come out from among us. Jesus talks about His separating us from the world in His prayer in the garden on the night of His betrayal:

JOHN 17:6-9-11-14-17 — I have manifested thy name unto the men which thou gavest me out of the world: thine they were and thou gavest them me: and they kept thy word. (9) I pray for them: I pray not for the world, but for them which thou has given me; for they are thine. (11) Now I am no more in the world, but these are in the world, and I come to thee. Holy Father, keep it through thine own name those whom thou hast given me, that they may be one, as we are. (14-17) I have given them thy word; and the world hath hated them, because they are not of the world, even as I am not of the world. I pray

not that thou shouldest take them out of the world, but that thou shouldest keep them from the evil. They are not of the world, even as I am not of the world. Sanctify them through thy truth: thy word is truth.

How clear it is here the difference the entrance of God's Holy Spirit into us makes us - and its consequences. So much so the people of the unsaved world see the difference in us but does not understand what makes the difference and as a result will have nothing to do with us. And in many cases do their best to eliminate us from the world by killing us. Yes God does expect a difference. He makes that difference - see:

<u>ROMANS 12:2</u> — Be not conformed to this world; but be Ye transformed by the renewing of your mind, that Ye may prove what is that good, and acceptable, and perfect, will of God.

<u>2 CORINTHIANS 6:17</u> — Wherefore come out from among them, and be Ye separate, saith the Lord, and touch not the unclean thing: and I will receive you.

<u>JAMES 4:4</u> — Ye adulterers and adulteresses, know Ye not that the friendship of the world is enmity with God? Whosoever therefore will be a friend of the world is the enemy of God.

The fact that you do come out and are separated from the world is good evidence that God is at work in you through that new nature He has put in you. Without that new nature giving us a better prospective of right and wrong we would not know any better than the rest of the world what is good and what is evil. But the entrance of God's nature in us has made us an altogether new creature that can understand good and evil much clearer than those without. This is made clear in:

2 CORINTHIANS 5:17 — **Therefore if any man be in Christ, he is a new creature: old things are passed away; behold, all things are become new.**

If a person confesses to be born again yet lives on in the manner of his former self in the love of the world - then on the authority of scripture - that person is telling a lie - or at best deceived himself, thinking he to be saved but in reality is not.

HOW GOD WORKS TO SEPARATE US:

In the next scripture we will read we will see how God works, the preordained method God uses to separate us from the world, and the purpose for which He separated us for:

2 PETER 1:2 — **Elect according to the foreknowledge of God the father, through sanctification of the Spirit, unto obedience and sprinkling of the blood of Jesus Christ: Grace unto you, and peace, be multiplied.**

Here it tells us plainly we are sanctified by God according to those plans we learned about earlier - the plans made for His elect way back in eternity past and finalized at His determinate counsel before He ever made this universe - through the separating of our spirit (not our physical body) - unto obedience!!

He had a purpose for His separating us - and gives us no choice in the matter. He separated us for the purpose of obedience - and we will be. Not 100% perfect, but still followers of Him as "born again" believers!!

God has a purpose for separating us. It was His initiative in separating based on His intentions to do so as far back in eternity as He Himself has existed - and that has been forever. This is what is referred to as God's foreknowledge. His intentions or purpose from eternity past even before they were finalized at His determinate counsel.

It is God who seeks us out in our lifetime. We would certainly never have come to Him unless He had sought us out. That is clear from:

ROMANS 3:10-17 — **As it is written, there is none righteous, no, not one: there is none that understandeth, there is none that seeketh after God. They are all gone out of the way, they are together become unprofitable; there is none that doeth good, no, not one. Their throat is an open sepulcher; with their tongues they have used deceit; the poison of asps is under their lips: whose mouth is full of cursing and bitterness: their feet are swift to shed blood: destruction and misery are in their ways: and the way of peace have they not known: there is no fear of God before their eyes.**

Not a very pretty picture is it? But that is the way we are - not one bit of interest in God in our human status. It is not until God enters us (sanctifies us through quickening us and we become born anew with God's Holy Spirit) that we become interested in God and all His truths. One may be religious before this - and be very zealous for that religion - but when God's Holy Spirit enters us all that will change. Our zeal will now be directed toward the true God. Then in:

CORINTHIANS 2:14 — **But the natural man receiveth not the things of the Spirit of God: for they are foolishness unto him; neither can he know them, because they are spiritually discerned.**

Spiritually discerned - just void of any capability of understanding or grasping unto anything of a spiritual nature. These verses clearly state our human inability to make a move towards God - in fact any move that is made by our own human nature is away from God. Even the Old Testament tells us of our inability to grasp unto the things of God. Let's go to:

Isaiah 64:6-8 - **We are all as an unclean thing, and all our righteousness are as filthy rags; and we all do fade as a leaf; and our iniquities, like the wind, have taken us away. And there is none that calleth upon thy name, that**

stirreth up himself to take hold of thee; for thou hast hid thy face from us, and has consumed us, because of our iniquities. But now, O Lord, thou are our father; we are the clay, and thou our potter; and we all are the work of they hands.

There is none that stirs himself up to call on God. Instead God calls us. He is the potter and we are the clay that God forms as He wishes. Both saved and unsaved. In our own human nature there dwells no good - therefore there can no good come from us - or expected to come from us of God.

This is all re-affirming what we already read in **Ephesians 2.** We live as the world does - enjoying the things the world does because we are of the world.

UNLESS

UNLESS God steps in and changes things in us and for us. How? Let's look at **Ezekiel 36:26-27** again.

EZEKIEL 36:26-27 — A new heart also will I give you, and a new spirit will I put within you: and I will take away the stony heart out of your flesh, and I will give you an heart of flesh.

I will put my spirit within you, and cause you to walk in my statutes, and Ye shall keep my judgments, and do them. God promises to give us a new spirit - that new spirit will cause us to believe - to be obedient to the demands of God. In addition - God has offered a sacrifice that would bear the punishment that God must metes out on those who disobey His commandments.

And that is every one of us. Every one of us must answer to God for where we fail to keep His law - without failing once in our whole life. If we fail in this standard of conduct we have 2 choices.

1) Spend in eternity in hell as punishment for our being a lawbreaker

or:

2) accept by God given faith what the lord Jesus Christ has done for us - His works which is the satisfaction of God's demands including the punishment for failing to keep them. Someone must be punished for our sins - ourselves, or a substitute. The Lord Jesus Christ is the only one who qualifies that can be your substitute. If you do His works will be applied to your credit - and your status will change from a condemned sinner to a justified believer!! FORGIVEN!!

Still a sinner in reality - but Justified by what the Lord Jesus Christ has done for you - everything God demands be done for a person to get to heaven. This being done - our salvation is a result of faith in what Jesus has done for us exactly as it says in Ephesians 2. Let's read it:

<u>EPHESIANS 2:8-10</u> — For by grace are Ye saved through faith; and that not of yourselves; it is the gift of God; Not of works, lest any man should boast. For we are his workmanship created in Christ Jesus unto God that we should walk in them.

Note as always the emphasis on our own efforts being of no value - but instead we are God's workmanship and He makes us as He pleases. If we only understood this we would not get so caught up in the law that we become dependent on that law for salvation. We have already read one scripture that makes this plain - so lets go to:

<u>ROMANS 9:17-24</u> — For the scripture saith unto Pharaoh, even for this same purpose have I raised thee up, that I might shew my power in thee, and that my name might be declared throughout all the earth. Therefore hath He mercy on whom he will have mercy, and whom He will He hardeneth. Thou wilt say then unto me, Why doth He yet find fault? For who hath, resisted his will? Nay but, O man, who art thou that

repliest against God? Shall the thing formed say to him that formed it, Why hast thou made me thus. Hath not the potter power over the clay, for the same lump to make one vessel unto honor, and another unto dishonor? What if God, willing to shew His wrath, and to make this power known, endured with much long suffering the vessels of wrath fitted to destruction: And that He might make known the riches of His glory on the vessels of mercy, which He had afore prepared unto glory. Even us, whom He hath called, not of the Jews only, but also of the Gentiles?

This is an incredibly important portion of scripture. It tells of God raising (in fact ordaining) pharaoh for the part he played in the story of Moses - how it was He **(GOD)** who hardened Pharaoh's heart and for the purpose He did that. He goes on to admonish those who rebel against this teaching of ordaining even sin and asks the question has not God got the power to do with His creation what He wants to? To make one pot (or person) for the purpose of salvation and another pot (person) for the purpose of condemnation. All this clay that He made the pots from came from the same lump of clay - mankind.

In review - what have we learned from the study of sanctification? Let's go back to the beginning - **Hebrews 10**:

HEBREWS 10:14 - For by one offering He hath perfected for ever them that are sanctified.

That's us!! Those of us who are trusting in the Lord Jesus and His works enabling us to get to heaven.

We must have learned that:

1) sanctification is the work of God in us that separates us from the way of life of the world about us.
2) That we are a peculiar people who think, act and talk much differently than the rest of the world..
3) We have learned that our separation from the world comes about

by the entering in of God's Holy spirit Which activates a new life - or nature within us. This action is called by three terms in the Bible.
    (i) quickened
    (ii) being born again.
    (iii) being regenerated

4) We learned that this new spirit that has been born within us acts as a new nature and has a great influence on the way we think, talk and act toward God, and that this change in our lifestyle is pretty sound evidence that God has indeed quickened us and sanctified us (set us apart) for some purpose or other we will find out before too long. This is clear as we read in:

<u>1 JOHN 3:9-10</u> — Whosoever abided in Him doth not commit sin; for His seed remaineth in Him: and he CANNOT sin, because he is born of God. In this the children of God are manifest, and the children of the devil: whosoever doeth not righteousness is not of God, neither he that loveth not his brother.

    Whoever is born of God does not live a life of sin. Everyone has their failures, but having a failure due to the weakness the flesh is a lot different than living a life of sin with no consciousness of his sinful ways. It goes on to say the way you can tell if a man is "born of God" or not is manifested (or shown - or demonstrated) by the fact of whether He lives a righteous life according to the laws of God - OR NOT. If he does not live a righteous life then that person is not born of God. If he does live a life that is based on the Bible and God's laws, than that demonstrates that he has God's Holy Spirit living in him. In other words - he has been born again.
    That is clear - how can we argue the point? Note something here: this does not necessarily mean living the law only - it means believing the "all things" taught in scripture. In fact the Bible makes it clear that believing all the doctrines of Christ is more important than keeping all the laws there is to keep just for the sake of keeping them thinking they will help you in some way get you in

better favor with God. Living the law as a lifestyle (because that is the way you want to live because God in you is causing you to think that way) is evidence you have God in you but in no way does any thing to help you on your road to heaven.

It is much better to believe all the doctrines of Christ - this demonstrates that God's Holy Spirit is in you more than anything else. And if you do have God's Holy Spirit in you He will influence you to keep the laws of God better than you could ever force yourself to do. The difference is God in you causes you to keep them - if you just do it for laws sake then it is just you doing them. That is not a sign that God is in you. But when you show belief in ALL the doctrines of God PLUS good works then that is very solid evidence of being born again.

Example: when Jesus told the scribes and Pharisees they needed to have better works than they had what did He mean? How could that be when humanly speaking they were about the best, cleanest living people on earth? It was because there works was of human ability for a show to the world. Don't forget what we have studied about one sin making us a guilty sinner - these Jewish leaders had sinned somewhere along the line just like any other man so these men were in need of a Saviour just as much as any other man. Jesus demanded a work that came from the influence of the Holy Spirit in them. For their salvation He demanded of them the only righteousness God recognizes - the righteousness of Jesus Christ imputed to them - just like all everyone else.

5) We have learned that those born of God has God's seed planted in him - such as the above verse says. He has been born of the seed of God. He now has a new nature born in him - which is another way of saying he has been born again. A second nature - not a renewed, or renovated nature as some would have us believe. We read in: **Romans 7:14-25** and again in **Galatians 5:17** of the conflict between these two natures. So it must be two natures. If it was just one nature that had been changed to a little better nature it could not fight against itself. We already have these two portions of scriptures recorded in this article so we will not repeat it here. But I suggest you read these and get it

clear in your mind that God does not touch the old nature - He adds a new one that lives alongside our old nature - and they are by no means friends. One - our human nature wants only to continue pleasing the flesh - the other nature - God's - wants to do that which is pleasing to God.

No - the Bible is clear - our old human nature stays as is. It stays as anti-God as ever and will continue to rebel against God and will be for as long as we are in the flesh - a torment and trouble maker. Why do you think even the most Godly of Christians can change quite quickly from a pious, highly respected Christian acting person to a person who you wouldn't want to introduce to a friend as a Christian in his present state. We all have our times that we are ashamed of. Why? Because we still have a human nature with the human failures that come with it that at the least provocation rears its ugly head - to our shame.

When God has something special He wants to accomplish He will put it in the mind of that person to do what God wants him to do and lo and behold what God wanted done will be done and most of the time the individual will not even know God was working out His pre-ordained will through him! God's thoughts will always over rule man's rebellious thoughts when God wants something done.

CLOSING THOUGHTS:

We have learned a lot of God and how He works. Let's close with these observations. Let's read:

JUDE 1:1-2 — Jude, the servant of Jesus Christ, and brother of James, TO THEM THAT ARE SANCTIFIED BY GOD THE FATHER, and PRESERVED IN JESUS CHRIST, and called: —— Mercy unto you, and peace, and love, be multiplied.

Here Jude in his salutation of his letter wishes those whom God has sanctified - or set apart for His personal use, and not only set apart but also preserved - or kept saved, and of course those who are the called - to those special people God chose, may mercy, peace and love be multiplied.

I will wish in my closing statement the same kind of people of our day these same great blessings.

LET'S SUMMARIZE SANCTIFICATION:

We see in scripture there are three stages of God's sanctifying us.

1) We were set apart in eternity past in the mind and purpose of God. He knew what He was going to do as far back in eternity as He Himself has existed - forever in past eternity. But He had not acted on those thoughts yet.

2) God starts to take action on what He had in mind all along. He Starts to put His thoughts into a formal plan I like to call a blue print form just for ease of under standing the difference between His thoughts and purpose and a formal plan. The plans become finalized at His determinate counsel. He is now ready to start carrying out that plan. The setting apart of His elect are part of that plan.

3) In each of their individual life those whom God had set apart for his special (peculiar) people He seeks out and separates from the world. He does not separate them physically from the world but in every other way we are. We look the same - but we sure don't think, talk, or act the same as we used to or the rest of the world does. We are different - distinct from the world and its ungodly system.

If you are not - you should examine your profession very closely. I hope each and every reader has had this great blessing of being sanctified for the Savior's use. All are not pastors or missionaries - but whatever position God calls you to be thankful and carry your commission out in a way that honors the one who commissions you.

ETERNAL SECURITY

ETERNAL SECURITY

By: David A. Shortt

Our subject this lesson is Eternal security.
The words eternal security are never found in the Bible - but the teaching of ones eternal security certainly is. Other words for it is -"once saved always saved". Better still - perseverance of the saints. Eternal Security means that once we are born of God - that is - that God's holy nature has been born within us giving us a second nature and that new nature will influence us to do good - that new nature will stay in us the rest of our life influencing us to live a better life style than we ever could other wise - not perfect as long as we are in the flesh - but better by far than if we did not have that second, holy nature living in us.

To get an understanding of what or why we must be eternally saved we must have an under standing of just where salvation comes from - our own good works or strictly through what our Lord did for us. If our salvation did depend on our own works - our own stirring up ourselves to grasp on God and confess Him of our own volition - then yes we would be in control of whether we accept Jesus or not - or whether we keep professing Him as Savior later on. If our salvation depended on how good our works were - how closely we followed all the laws of God then of course if we failed and made a mess of our lives and broke the laws time after time we would lose our salvation as a penalty for breaking those laws our salvation depended on by keeping them.

Where all this theory fails is the fact that our salvation does NOT depend on our making our own decision about accepting Jesus as Savior - or how well we keep the law. Our salvation then must depend on someone who has kept the law in its entirety and imputes His righteousness to us who will trust in that righteousness imputed to us - that of the Lord Jesus Christ. Understanding the doctrines of election, predestination, the sovereignty of God, the depravity of man all helps understand eternal security - they all fit in with each other.

We have studied enough about this subject I think to have it clear in our mind that our salvation is strictly what God, Jesus and the Holy Spirit has done and is doing in us so there is no need of going over that. Just in a very short review - remember **James 2:10** tells us if we fail to keep one of God's laws - His standard of conduct - then as far as God is concerned we break them all - continuously. Therefore we must look to someone outside our mere human capabilities to some one who can and already has lived up to the standard God requires and is willing to impute His righteousness to those who believe - or trust that He kept it for them personally. That person is Jesus Christ - he kept the law for us. So now we believers trust in what Jesus has done for us and we are under the righteousness of Jesus and we will be safe and secure under this protection as long as the Lord Jesus himself shall exist. Eternally. Read:

Romans 8:28-39: — **We know that all things work together for good to them that love God, to them who are the called according to his purpose. For whom He did foreknow, He also did predestinate to be conformed to the image of His Son, that He might be the firstborn among many brethren. Moreover whom He did predestinate, them He also called: and whom He called, them He also justified: and whom He justified, them He also glorified. What shall we then say to these things? If God be for us, who can be against us? He that spared not His own Son, but delivered Him up for us all, how shall He**

not with Him also freely give us all things? Who shall lay any thing to the charge of God's elect? It is God that justifieth. Who is He that condemneth? It is Christ that died, yea rather, that is risen again, who is even at the right hand of God, who also maketh intercession for us. Who shall separate us from the love of Christ? Shall tribulation, or distress, or persecution, or famine, or nakedness, or peril, or sword? As it is written, For thy sake we are killed all the day long; we are accounted as sheep for the slaughter. Nay, in all these things we are more than conquerors through him that loved us. For I am persuaded, that neither death, nor life, nor angels, nor principalities, nor powers, nor things present, nor things to come, Nor height, nor depth, nor any other creature, shall be able to separate us from the love of God, which is in Christ Jesus our Lord.

This gives us an insight of God's plan way back into eternity past.

God has known as long as He himself has existed - and that as been forever - what He was going to do. Then on the basis of this knowing "what He is going to do" (called His foreknowledge) He goes ahead and makes up His blue print for life & time. This He did at His determinate counsel. It was here God put all the plans He had in His foreknowledge - The knowledge of what He was going to do all through His existence - into blue print form. The plans were all made out and determined exactly what would happen in time. Then He puts those plans into motion and today we are still living those plans out. This determinate counsel is mentioned in:

<u>**Acts 2:23**</u> — **Him, being delivered by the determinate counsel and foreknowledge of God, Ye have taken, and by wicked hands have crucified and slain.**

We see from this that God knew from all eternity as long as He existed that He knew what He was going to do - who He would save - who He wouldn't save. Therefore it can be understood that our salvation has been secure as far back into eternity as God Himself existed and will be as secure as God is as far out into future eternity God exists.

This determinate counsel, as we can see by its very name, is where all things were determined. Nothing in this creation happens that were not determined at that counsel. Since our salvation does not depend on what we say or do, but what God, Jesus and the Holy Ghost does for and in us - then our salvation is secure as long as the Godhead will exist. I am pretty sure we all will agree that will be forever. Read:

1 Corinthians 2:5 — That your faith should not stand in the wisdom of men, but in the power of God.

This we should understand - our salvation stands in the power of God - not of us or anything we can think or do. Further evidence of our security being in God working in us is found in:

1 John 3:9 — Whosoever is born of God doth not commit sin; for his seed remaineth in him: and he cannot sin, because he is born of God. In this the children of God are manifest, and the children of the devil: whosoever doeth not righteousness is NOT of God, neither he that loveth not his brother.

What evidence is there that one has NOT been born of this new nature. The best evidence of course is that they don't continue on in a Christian walk (especially believing in Jesus Christ for salvation - not their own works) - or don't follow the laws and are not obedient to God and His instructions as found in the Holy Bible.
Read:

1 John 2:19 — They went out from us, but they were not of us; for if they had been of us, they would no doubt have continued with us: but they went out, that they might be made manifest that they were not all of us.

Conversely - the evidence that one HAS been born of God is when they DO hear and follow God and trusts Jesus and are obedient to God's laws and instructions in righteousness - not FOR salvation - but BECAUSE of a work in their heart by the Holy Spirit living in them. Jesus in John 8:47 makes it clear That those who will believe and follow Him - those who are of God (or taught by God) - those are the ones who have the Holy spirit dwelling in them, and will follow Him in a obedience. If they do not have the Holy Spirit dwelling in them - they can not live an obedient life to God.

John 8:47 — He that is of God heareth God's words: Ye therefore hear them not, because Ye are not of God.

John 5:24 — Verily, verily, I say unto you, He that hearth my word, and believeth on Him that sent me, HATH ever lasting life, and shall not come into condemnation; but is passed from death unto life.

Those who DO believe all ready HAS eternal life in them. They do NOT get eternal life by believing as taught by most religions.
Note closely the next two verses.

John 6:29 — Jesus answered and said unto them, This is the work of God, that Ye believe on him whom He hath sent.

Note here that believing is a work of God. Now let's look at the next scripture.

Ecclesiastes 3:14 — I know that, whatsoever God doeth, it shall be for ever: nothing can be put to it, nor any thing taken from it: and God doth it, that men should fear before him.

We noted in **John 6:39** that a person believing is the work of God. In the second scripture we note that whatever God does it shall be for ever. If this is true then when God causes us to believe by the work of the Holy Spirit working in us then it will be forever. This is the difference between believing in our own works which can be very temporary and believing in God's work which is forever. More on our security in Jesus -

John 6:37 to 47 and 54 — **all that the Father giveth me shall come to me; and him that cometh to me I will in no wise cast out. For I came down from heaven, not to do mine own will, but the will of him that sent me. And this is the Father's will which hath sent me, that of all which he hath given me I should lose nothing, but should raise it up again at the last day. And this is the will of Him that sent me, that every one which seeth the son, and believeth on him, hath have everlasting life: and I will raise him up at the last day. The Jews then murmured at him, because he said, I am the bread of life which came down from heaven. And they said, Is not this Jesus, the son of Joseph whose father and mother we know? How is it then that he saith, I came down from heaven? Jesus therefore answered and said unto them, Murmur not among yourselves. No man can come to me, except the Father which hath sent me draw him: and I will raise him up at the last day. It is written in the prophets, and they shall be all taught of (by) God. Every man therefore that hath heard, and hath learned of (by) the Father, cometh unto me. Not that any man hath seen the Father, save he which is of (taught by) God, he hath seen the Father. Verily, verily, I say unto you, He that believeth on me hath (already has) everlasting life.   Verse 54: Whoso eateth my flesh, and drinketh my blood, hath (already has) eternal life; and I will raise him up at the last day.**

And finally let's look at these scriptures:

John 6:65 to 69 — **And He said, therefore said I unto you, that no man can come unto me, except it were given unto him of my Father. From that time many of his disciples**

went back, and walked no more with Him. Then said Jesus unto the twelve, will Ye also go away? Then Simon Peter answered him, Lord, to whom shall we go? Thou hast the words of eternal life. And we believe and are sure that thou art that Christ, the son of the living God.

This summarizes up all that has been said. No man can come unless God enables one by the work of the Holy Spirit in us. I wish every one that reads this can say the same as what Peter said here. "And we believe and are sure that thou are that Christ, the son of the living God.
If you can you also will spend eternity with God.

<u>Hebrews 12:2</u> — Looking unto Jesus the author and finisher of our faith; who for the joy that was set before Him endured the cross, despising the shame, and is set down at the right hand of the throne of God. Salvation is of God: the author and finisher of our faith.

(I like to paraphrase that to read - 'the author of our faith - and all the way to the finish of our faith.')
It has all to do with God - therefore our salvation will endure as long as God the father , God the son, and God the Holy Ghost will exist – **ETERNALLY!!!**

God bless.

THIS ENDS THIS SERIES OF LESSONS

1. David A. Shortt was born in Englehart Ontario. This is still a small village tucked away in a very fertile valley about 300 miles north of Toronto. Mr. Shortt left the north country at sixteen to get work in Hamilton Ontario. Work was scarce and not getting a job he joined the Navy - a career he had always been interested in any way. While in the Navy he met with Christians on board ship that led him to meet a pastor in San Juan P.R. He came to know the Lord at that time, was Baptized and became a confirmed Baptist. The last ten years or so He has been unable to work so he took to writing Christian doctrinal books. Some of these books are: **My Stand on the doctrines of Grace, The Sovereignty of God, The Church that Jesus built, Basic Studies in Soteriology, Calvinism or Arminianism?, The Baptist are Jesus' Church, The Cross.** With more being written at this time. You are invited to search them out and read them.
2. This book takes a close look at the doctrines of soterliogy from its beginning action when God enters the heart of a person in regeneration through the resulting conversion of the individual, explaining the meaning of sanctification and how God does set apart a people for him and God's taking care of His saints until the final Roll call when His people meet with God in His heavenly Kingdom.

Printed in the USA
CPSIA information can be obtained
at www.ICGtesting.com
LVHW091312161123
763810LV00091B/539